The Duties of the Heart

By Rabbi Ben Joseph Ibn Bachye

Translated by Edwin Collins

Hellier Hebrew Scholar, University College, London

PANTIANOS
CLASSICS

Published by Pantianos Classics

ISBN-13: 978-1-78987-497-6

First published in 1905

Contents

Editorial Preface

The object of the editors of this series is a very definite one. They desire above all things that, in their humble way, these books shall be the ambassadors of good-will and understanding between East and West, the old world of Thought, and the new of Action. In this endeavour, and in their own sphere, they are but followers of the highest example in the land. They are confident that a deeper knowledge of the great ideals and lofty philosophy of Oriental thought may help to a revival of that true spirit of Charity which neither despises nor fears the nations of another creed and colour. Finally, in thanking press and public for the very cordial reception given to the "Wisdom of the East" series, they wish to state that no pains have been spared to secure the best specialists for the treatment of the various subjects at hand.

L. Cranmer-Byng.

S. A. Kapadia.

Introduction

BACHYE'S "Guide to the Duties of the Heart" is the unique work that first linked the ethical science of the West with the emotional and spiritual morality of the East. It combines, in an artistic unity, elements drawn from the philosophy and contemplative mysticism of the Arabs, from Biblical and Rabbinic Judaism, and from Greek thought. By exhibiting the spiritual foundations of universal Ethics, and of the moral law of the Bible, in the light of pure reason, Bachye prepared the way for finding that common ground on which, wholly or in part, all the moral religions, and all the non-religious systems of morality, are rooted. Therefore, although actually written in Spain, a land of the West, it forms a fitting opening volume for the "Wisdom of the East Series."

Only a small part of the original finds a place in the following pages; but I have in my translation — sometimes literal, now and again a summarised pharaphrase — endeavoured to give a selection of passages connected by the author's central thought, and showing his line of argument and the aim and spirit of his work, instead of a mere collection of pithy sayings and isolated, beautiful, but disconnected reflections. This was the only way of doing justice to an author, some of whose reasonings are out of date, but the spirit of whose main contention is eternally valid; a teacher of virtue and duty, who did not attempt to inculcate this or that individual virtue, but aimed at the formation of character and conditions in which right conduct would be inevitable, so that details might well be left to take care of themselves.

If the modern world owes its delight in physical beauty, and much of its sense of the true in Nature and in Art, to Greece; its ideal of goodness, and practically all the spiritual elements in our thought and feeling, our conception of holiness, and every moral characteristic of civilisation and of culture, have come to us from the Orient. For the form and system of Ethics we may be indebted to the few Hellenic thinkers whose sublime intellects raised them above the phenomenal world into a clear atmosphere of ideas, always suffused with the light of truth and justice; but all the permanent and vital contents of Ethics came, living and pulsating, with their vitalising possibilities, both into that atmosphere and into our life of to-day, with the glow of dawn from the East. Indeed, the two cardinal ideas essential to all present and future moral systems — the sanctity of human life as such, and the absolutely universal authority and validity of moral law and obligation — are entirely absent from even the writings of Plato, the greatest of the Greeks. These two are among the most definite colours that the prism of modern thought has enabled us to single out in our perception of the pure white light, from the sun of righteousness, that shone on Sinai. They are specially characteristic of the Hebrew moral teaching which the three great religions — Judaism, Christianity and Islamism — have spread throughout the world.

In the world's organism, it seems to be the special function of the Oriental peoples to secrete, or to absorb from what is, or may be, beyond and above the physical universe, all that man needs to nourish the life of his soul and to perfect his individuality; while it is the function of the Western civilised nations to show the Eastern peoples how the material resources and the forces of nature may be mastered, and the observed relations which we call nature's laws may be applied to serve the purposes of material life, individual and communal. The Semitic religious, and the Aryan-Oriental mystic, intuitions, seem to be the chlorophyll that draws, from the sunlight of spiritual being, elements essential to the healthy growth of the human race; and if Western humanity is to be saved from becoming a dry and sapless log, it must perennially renew that foliage which brings it into contact with the ambient upper air, warmed by the glow of righteousness and love.

It is to help in this process of renewing the spiritual and moral life of the West that the "Orient Press" is publishing the present series of selections.

In the middle and latter half of the eleventh century, Spain became the rallying-point, and a radiating centre, of Jewish culture — religious, philosophical, and poetic; and while practically the whole of the Western world was then sunk in the intellectual darkness of the Middle Ages, the Jews of Spain were not only cultivating the sciences and developing, to its highest perfection, their own spiritual and intellectual heritage; they were also preparing the way for the Renaissance, and for the re-enfranchisement of Western thought, by their study, and dissemination, in Hebrew and Arabic translations, of the philosophy of Greece. It was the Jews of Spain who were the chief students of the so-called Arabian philosophy, and the chief instruments by whom it was subsequently made effective on European culture. "It was," says Lewes, in his "History of Philosophy," "through their translators, and through their original thinkers, such as Avicebron [Jehudah Ibn Gebirol, the author of the "Vons Vitae," *b.* 1021; *d.* 1070], and Moses Maimonides, that the West became leavened with Greek and Oriental thought."

It is to this brilliant period in the history of Jewish literature that our author belongs.

Rabbi Bachye bar Joseph ibn Bakoda was a contemporary of the poet-philosopher Ibn Gebirol, and held, in the Jewish community, the position of Dayan — an office which combines something of the duties of a judge in civil, religious, and matrimonial causes, with those of a Rabbi authorised to answer questions on all matters of Jewish law and life, and on the application, to special and exceptional cases, of the general principles found in the Bible and Talmud.

Next to nothing is known of his life, and even the exact date of his birth, and the place where he held office, are not known with certainty. The evidence, however, seems in favour of Jellinek's opinion that he lived in Saragossa, was born in the second half of the eleventh century, and died in the first half of the twelfth century.

He was a man of the most amiable and genial character, and, though profoundly religious, extremely liberal-minded. He was an industrious student of all the science of his day, and held it to be a sacred duty to gain, both by observation and by independent thought, a knowledge, as complete as possible, of the material world and of the history of man. Believing that every accession to our knowledge, and every strengthening of our instrument of thought, must tend to deepen our admiration for the Creator, and tend to fit us more and more thoroughly for fulfilling the ideal of our *raison d'être*, and, by perfecting our character, tend to perfect us in our worldly conduct and in our relations with our fellow-men; he held it to be a moral and religious duty to study what are usually called secular subjects. Thus natural science, mathematics, anthropology, zoology, history, etc., etc., are numbered by him among the matters with which the seeker after spiritual and moral truth is bound to occupy himself. He teaches also, by his own example, as well as by express injunction, the duty of "learning from everybody, no matter to what race or creed he may belong," no matter what may be his religious opinions.

Before the writing of his "Duties of the Heart," no systematic treatise on Ethics had appeared among the Jews. Hebrew literature, from the Bible onwards, is, of course, full of ethical and moral teaching, and the same must be said of the Talmud and the Midrashim, "The Sentences of the Fathers," and of Rabbi Nathan; while "The Masecheth Derech Eretz," Ibn Gebirol's "The Choicest of the Pearls," and "The Son of Proverbs," by Samuel Hannagid, must be mentioned among the chief works with ethical contents. But no scientific working out of a system of ethics based on one central thought, and claiming universal validity, had even been thought of. Bachye also complained that although there was no lack of guidance as to the duties of the body and its members, by which he understood all the outward conduct of life — even honesty in dealing, deeds of charity and benevolence and even the activities of the tongue and lips in prayer and praise, and in good or evil speaking, in telling the truth and in lying — there was no book dealing with the Duties of the Heart and Mind.

It was to supply this want that he wrote, in Arabic, the book which was destined in its Hebrew Translation [1] to become one of the most popular as well as the most authoritative expositions of spiritual Judaism. This work has never appeared in English.

By the Duties of the Heart Bachye understands the whole of conduct, and of thought in its ideal essence. For he holds that the outward act is, morally, of no significance, except in so far as it represents a manifestation of character and an expression of intention.

The whole of conduct belongs to the domain of ethics. Every act, and every abstention from action, is either right or wrong. Even the amount one eats, the wearing of certain clothes, the use of language, the simplest movements of the body, are, all of them, parts of conduct to be distinguished as either right or wrong. But what makes them so is *not* the act itself, but the intention with which it is done or left undone. And, since our intentions are conditioned by our state of mind and feeling, the first and the final duty, the foundation of ethics, is the perfection of our own souls.

Thus Bachye is at one with Stephen in asserting that "the moral law has to be asserted in the form: not 'do this,' but 'be this.'"

The perfection of the human soul, however, from which all right conduct must result, and which every righteous act and every righteous thought tends to produce, is only attained by bringing it into complete unison with God, through such a perfect love of Him that His will is our will, and we have no desire that is out of harmony with His wisdom and His benevolence.

But Bachye's ethics is not theological in the sense of taking as its starting-point the Bible, or any other revelation or authoritative statement of the will of God, who can only be known through His works, the universe and man, who is the world in miniature (the microcosm). He does not even take for granted the existence of a God at all, nor appeal to revelation for assertion of that truth. He starts *ab initio*, and claims to deal with the problems of absolute being by the aid of reason and — note well — *observation of the material world.*

He starts by submitting to the test of reason the questions, — "Is there a Creator or not?" and if so, "Is there more than one Creator?" and "What can we know about Him?"

He then proceeds to demonstrate the duty of devoting the heart and mind to the study and contemplation of the works of God, whence conviction of the infinite goodness of the Creator, and of the infinite indebtedness, and obligation to gratitude, of the creature, are borne in upon the mind.

Contemplation of the results of such study will lead to true humility, and to perfect trust in God and resignation to His will, devotion to His service and the concentration (unification) of all works on His service. This service does not mean religious observance, though it may, and in the case of Israelites must, include it; but means the doing of His will and ethical conduct. Asceticism is recommended as a means of removing hindrances to union with God.

Full intellectual recognition of the goodness of the Creator will, through gratitude and humility, lead to perfect and disinterested love of God and

an understanding of His will, which includes benevolence to all creatures. Hence this love of God
will suffice, without rewards or punishments,
even without the commands of the Bible or of
human legislation, to induce perfect conduct in
every relation of life. The restraints and commands of the Bible are given to bring the less intelligent of mankind this; but, being of divine
origin, the Law will also be accepted as *part* of
their duty by those who reach ethical conduct and
feeling through reason; and such of them as are
Israelites will keep the specially Jewish laws. Thus
the obligation to right conduct is not Jewish but
universal, and valid for all reasonable beings as
creatures; and the contemplation of the one infinite cause of good takes the place of the contemplation of the idea of justice. The specially Jewish
obligations are only binding on Jews, and the
higher obligations of philosophic contemplation
only on those gifted with exceptional mental
powers. So that all men can be equally meritorious — the Jew, the heathen, the philosopher, and
the fool or slave — since each perfectly fulfils the
will of God *as it applies to him,* and pays *in full* his
debt of gratitude, small or great.

The ethical system of Bachye is distinctly Oriental. All the impulse to virtuous conduct springs
from the point of contact between the human soul

and the unseen soul of the universe. It is the individual in communion with God, the creature bowed in awsome gratitude before the Creator, who recognises the obligations of ethical conduct; not the citizen seeking the best way to become a good citizen and preserve the State. Moreover, the development is not from the outer circle of sociological duties to the inner circle of the family, and the centre, the individual soul, as in Greek ethics; not from the circumference of deeds to the centre of ideals and soul perfection; but from the centre, the soul, to the outward act.

It is interesting to note that, although Bachye is an orthodox Rabbi, his ethics is not a Jewish theological work, but sets forth a motive to right conduct, starting from universal reason, and appealing, not only to the Children of Israel, nor even to the wise and intelligent alone, but to all mankind. Human reason is the ultimate test of conduct, of revelation, and of faith. The duties of the heart are more important than those of the body, because they are of universal application, and not limited by time, or place, or circumstance.

Edwin Collins.

Feb, 1, 1904.

[1] By Jehudah Ibn Tibbon.

The Duties of the Heart

Wisdom, the Highest Good

"THE supreme benefit, and the highest good bestowed by the Creator on human beings (after the gift of existence and the perfected faculties of perception and intelligence), is Wisdom. This, indeed, is the very life of their spirits. It is the lamp of their reason, which enables them to come to the will of God, and delivers them from all disaster in this world and in the world to come.

This Wisdom, or Philosophy, is of three kinds: the Philosophy of Nature, dealing with the properties and accidents of Matter; the Philosophy of Number and Measurement, the Mathematical Wisdom, including Astronomy and Music; and Philosophy, properly so called, including the knowledge of God, and the knowledge of His laws, and the rest of the sciences that are concerned with life and mind, and with human souls and spiritual beings. But all divisions of Wisdom are gates which the Creator, Blessed be He, has opened to human beings to enable them to attain to religion and the world. Only some of these sciences are more necessary to the subject of Religion, and other divisions are more necessary for the attainment of worldly advantage. The highest form of Wisdom, the Divine Wisdom, is that which is most necessary to Religion. It is our duty to study this philosophy, in order, by means of Reason and discriminating intelligence, to attain to our religion, to morality and the laws of life that make for the health of our bodies and our souls. [1]

Seek no Reward but Wisdom's Self

But it is forbidden to us to study it for purposes of worldly advantage; but from the single motive of Love Alone. The Rabbis say: "Do things for the sake of the work itself, and speak the words [of the law] for their own sake. Thou shalt neither make the Torah a crown, to magnify thyself with it, nor a spade to dig with." And they say, in reference to words of Psalm cxii., "'Happy is the man who fears the Eternal, and delighteth greatly in His Commandments,' Rabbi Eliezar explains 'delighteth greatly in His Commandments, themselves, and not in the merit, or in any reward, spiritual or material, attached to their performance, as we have learned,' 'be not like servants that serve their master for the sake of receiving a reward, but be ye like servants who serve their master with the intention of receiving no reward, and let the awe of Heaven be upon you.'"

Three gates the Creator has opened to mankind, so that they may enter into the domain of spirituality, ethical conduct and the laws divine, that guide us in our works and daily life to health of body and of mind and soul. The first is the lofty portal of pure Reason, with all obstructing errors cleared away; the second is the book of the Torah [2] revealed to Moses, the prophet; the third is built up of traditions.

The Ethics of the Body and the Ethics of the Soul

The wisdom of the *Torah* [2] is divided into two parts:

I. The wisdom of the visible, that enables us to know the duties of the body and its members; and these include not only all the practical obligations both of ethics and religion, but also all the physical obligations and restraints of a good and moral life.

II. The Duties of the Heart and Mind; duties that concern thought and feeling, and whose fulfilment is entirely in the hidden depths of the human heart and soul, and this is the wisdom of the invisible.

The duties of the heart and mind have all of them their roots in human reason, and, like some corporeal duties, would be recognised as binding even without revelation.

Examples of Duties of the Heart

Among commands relating to duties of the heart and mind are the following:— To believe that the world has a Creator, who created it from nothing, and that there is none other like Him. To accept His Unity and worship Him in our hearts. To devote intelligent thought to the wonders of His Creation, so that they may be to us a sign concerning Him. To trust in Him, and humble ourselves before Him; to fear Him, to tremble at the thought that He looks at us — at all that is revealed and all that is hidden about us; to desire to do His will; and to concentrate all our efforts upon good deeds that are absolutely disinterested and only motived by love of God. Further, that we should love Him and those that love Him, and hate those that hate Him.

Also, that we should not covet, and not avenge, or bear a grudge. (Compare Levit. xix.) They also forbid us to think sinful thoughts, or to have sinful desires, and even to contemplate the commission of any transgression, and other similar things which are hidden from man and none but God, alone, can see.

Thus the duties of the heart involve the formation of ideals of conduct, love of man, faith, etc.; the cultivation of right beliefs based upon Reason; the conscious effort of the mind to realise the wonders of creation, so that we may come to know, of God, truths which human language, that can only accurately tell of things material, can never adequately express. That trust in God which makes right conduct possible, even at the cost of personal risk and loss; the banishing of hatred, envy, scorn, all longing for revenge, and all desire for sin, are also obligations of the heart. And they include all nuances of virtue, such as these that have their being in the heart alone, and are not manifested in material life, save only by their influence; and yearning, till the yearning one turns pale with longing, [3] to realise, in thought and mind and deed, the will of God. And chief among them is the attuning of the soul into such perfect harmony with God, that all right conduct and right thought must follow without effort on our part, because our will is one with His, through love.

The Duties of the Heart are more Important than Any Others

The obligation to fulfil the duties of the heart and mind is greater than any other, for, whether they refer to the commands of Reason, or to those of Scripture or of Tradition, they are the foundations of all the precepts; and if there chance to be even the slightest failure in the ethics of the soul, there can be no proper fulfilment of any external ethical duty.

The Dual Duty of the Dual Man

Man is made up of body and soul; and both alike are given us by the beneficence of the Creator. The one is visible, and the other invisible. We are therefore bound to serve Him with a twofold service. That of the body and its members can be fulfilled by the visible activities of man; but the second is a hidden service, which is the fulfilment of the duties of the heart — to acknowledge the Unity of God in our hearts, to believe in Him, to love

Him, resign our souls to Him, and make His name the unifying central thought of all our conduct.

All Conduct is Conditioned by the Heart

It is quite clear to me that even the duties of the body and its members can never be perfectly fulfilled, except with a willing heart, and a soul that delights to do them, and when our heart is really full of yearning for the work that they involve. And should the thought arise in our minds that our moral obligation requires only outward acts of goodness, and that our hearts are not in duty bound to choose the service of The Infinite [4] and to delight in it, then the obligation to ethical conduct would also be removed from the body and its members. For no act of any kind is done completely unless the soul delights in doing it.

Moreover, with regard to any sinful conduct, it is not the act itself, but the sinful intention, by which one incurs guilt. It is only when the heart co-operates with the bodily members in the commission of an offence that guilt is incurred; so that it is the intention of the heart that is the principal element in either virtue or vice, and he who does a meritorious action unintentionally is still without merit. Thus the essential thing in all conduct is the intention of the heart.

The Duties of the Heart are for every Time and Place

While some religious and moral duties are only obligatory at special times and in special circumstances, these duties of the heart, taught by Reason, Scripture, or Tradition, are incumbent upon us continually, all the days of our life and at every moment. As the Psalmist says: — (Ps. cxix.) "Trust in the Eternal at all times." Nor, for instance, can there be a moment of our lives when it is not incumbent upon us to remove hatred and jealousy from our hearts.

Endless Virtues spring from those of the Heart

These inner virtues of the mind and heart, unlike the precepts that the body can fulfil, are not only very numerous themselves, but form the inexhaustible source of innumerable virtues and obligations.

The Duty of using Reason: and of taking no Dogma on Trust

It is the bounden duty of all who are not intellectually incapable of independent thought, to search out the true meaning of the doctrines they accept, and the foundations of these doctrines in Reason.

Faith without Knowledge

The faith of the believer is not complete unless he knows the meaning and the reasons of his belief. And this knowledge that enables one to fulfil the duties of the heart, is the hidden wisdom that is the light of hearts and the bright effulgence of souls; and concerning it Scripture says:—(Ps. li. 6) "Behold Thou desirest truth in the inward parts and in the hidden, Thou wilt make me to know wisdom." It is only those of weak intellect who are not culpable if they take on trust what it is man's duty to search out. But whoever has the strength of intellect, and the power to sift and prove, is sinful if he neglects to do so, and also even his lack of knowledge is a sin.

(From the Gate of Unity.)

Belief in the Existence of One Creator as the Basis of Ethics

Perfect recognition of the existence and unity of God forms the only sure basis for right thought and conduct. For gratitude to the beneficent Creator of the universe, and admiration of creation, involve the reasoned resolve to benefit all His creatures, study His works, and raise our souls, perfecting them; and tends to love of Him, resulting in obedience to His will, whether revealed through Nature or through human agency, or in our innate faculties for recognising justice and the good.

The love of God, and the consequent acceptance of the yoke of duty in obedience to His will, is, in the Scripture passage that strikes the key-note of the faith of Israel, placed after the injunction to understand that the Creator exists, that the Eternal is God, and that He is One. (Hear and understand, [5] O Israel, the Eternal is our God, the Eternal is One) (Deut. vi.).

The unity of conduct, and the concentration of our love and striving after good, require belief in One, and only one, Creator, the source of good.

The Examination of Creation shows the Goodness of the Creator

The way in which man can most readily arrive at a knowledge of God is by a critical study of the works of creation in general, and of man in particular.

The result of this examination will be to show you that the Creator is not only wise but infinitely good and beneficent, and that His goodness is over all His works.

(From The Third Gate, explaining the Obligation of Accepting the Service of the Deity, Blessed be He.)

Free Will and Providence

When you understand the mystery of movement and the dynamic laws of the universe, and realise how these, in their working, are among the greatest wonders of the wisdom of God, and you recognise how great has been the mercy of the Creator to His creatures in the operation of these laws, then it will be clear to you that all your movements are bound and controlled by the pleasure of the Creator, blessed be He, and His providence, and His will — the smallest and least important as well as the greatest, the obvious as well as those that are hidden — with one great exception: that He has placed in your power the choice of good and evil.

Gratitude to God and Man

Since Reason obliges us to do good to all who do good to us; a recognition of the existence and unity of God, and of His beneficence, shows the duty of serving Him.

Gratitude is due for Good Intentions

All admit that our obligation to benefactors is in proportion to their intention to benefit us, and that even if, through some accident or hindrance, their deeds fall short of their goodwill, and they fail to do us good; ...while, on the other hand, we owe no debt of gratitude to those by whose acts we are benefited without their intending to do us good. It will now be shown that while in almost all the motives to human benevolence self-interest plays a part, the benevolence of God is entirely disinterested.

The Motives of Human Benevolence

There are five aspects of human beneficence:— (1) that of the father to his children; (2) of the master to his slave; (3) of the rich to the poor, in order that he may receive the reward of heaven; (4) that of some men to others, for the sake of acquiring a good name, or honour, or worldly reward; (5) that of the strong towards the weak, because he pities them, and because he is pained on account of their condition.

If we look closely at all these kinds of benevolence, we shall find that, in motive, not one of them is entirely disinterested.

The beneficence of a father is for his own good. The son is a part of himself, and the very substance of his hope and his ambition. And do we not see that a father is more anxious about his children than about his own body — in regard to their food and drink and clothing, and in warding off all injuries from them; and the natural parental compassion and kindness of fathers for their children makes the burden of all trouble and labour, and all disturbance of his rest on behalf of his children, seem light to him.

Nevertheless, Reason, as well as Scripture, obliges the child to serve, honour, and reverence his parents.

And even though the parent is compelled, by the promptings of Nature, to all this, and although these natural instincts are of God, whose delegate in this respect he is, such honour and gratitude are no less due to him.

The beneficence of a master to his slave is prompted only by self-interest, and yet the Creator has made it the duty of the slave to repay that goodness with service and gratitude as well.

The beneficence of the rich to the poor, for the sake of the reward of heaven, is like the purchase by a business man of a great and permanent advantage to come to him at some future time, in return for a small, perishable, and contemptible good that he parts with immediately; and his only intention is to adorn his own soul in his after-life. And yet, in spite of all this, gratitude is due to him.

The beneficence of one section of mankind to another for the sake of the love of praise and honour and worldly reward, is like the conduct of a man who gives his neighbour goods to take care of until he wants them for himself, or who entrusts money to his neighbour which he will, himself, require later on. But although his intention is only to benefit himself in doing good to others, yet praise and gratitude are due to him.

Even he that takes pity upon the poor and the afflicted whose sufferings are painful to him, intends, by relieving them, to relieve himself of a pain that afflicts his own soul; and he is like one who, by the goodness of God, is healing himself of a painful illness; but yet he is not left without praise.

Thus the primary intention of everyone in doing good to others, is to do good to himself, or save himself from pain.

Man's Obligation of Gratitude to God

If man earns gratitude, reward and love for intermittent beneficence that is not unselfish, how great must be our obligation of service, gratitude and praise to the Creator of goodness, who there with causes all good, and whose goodness is without end and continuous, and is entirely free from all egoistic motive or intention, but is a pure freewill gift, and whose kindness is extended to all reasonable beings.

The Motive Forces that Impel Man to Grateful Service

There are two distinct motive forces impelling man to humble and grateful service of God. One of them is inherent in human reason, implanted in man's intelligence, and hidden deep within the very roots of his being; the second is acquired by means of his hearing and understanding. This second is the Torah. [6]

The service due to the humility of hope and fear is that which arises from the acquired, external motive which enforces the obligation with rewards and punishments in this world and in the world to come; the second kind is induced by the working of the hidden motive force of Reason, innate in human nature, and bound up with the union of man's soul to his body. Both kinds of humility are praiseworthy, and both lead to a right way of life and conduct; but the one is the complement of the other, and the motive of the Torah is the stepping-stone to both, while the motive of Reason, and the way of proof, is the preferable and nearer to God.

The service undertaken at the prompting of Reason is free from all suspicion of hypocrisy, and from all admixture of hope or fear. It springs from a philosophic knowledge of how the creature is indebted to the Creator, and is not restricted to actual outward acts, but will include the ethical working of the heart and mind — the fulfilment of the duties of the heart.

The Whole of Human Conduct belongs to the Domain of Ethics

The whole of human conduct may be divided into acts that are commanded and acts that are prohibited, and acts that are necessary to the maintenance of physical existence and that are just sufficient for human needs, such as eating, drinking, sufficient speech for the conduct of worldly affairs, and so forth. For every act that passes the boundary line of what is just sufficient, either tending to superfluity or to insufficiency, cannot escape from inclusion among acts commanded by Reason or by Scripture, if its intention be for the sake of God; or among prohibited acts, if its passing of the border line be not for the sake of God. [7] When, however, we examine more closely the kind of actions described as being neither commanded nor forbidden, but merely necessary to human life and the order of the world, we discover that it belongs to the category of things commanded from the very beginning of creation (here again Scripture and Reason — Ethics, properly so-called — are in agreement), for in Genesis we find:—"And God blessed them and said, be fruitful and multiply, and fill the earth and subdue it; and later on, "Thus behold I have given unto you every herb bearing seed which is upon the face of the earth for food." Thus the eating of sufficient food is also commanded in the Law, and since this is so, it is clear that every possible [intentional] action of the sons of men is either commanded or forbidden, and that he who does anything commanded (by Reason or Scripture) is performing a good deed, and if he leaves it undone, he has failed in his duty. And, in like manner, to do anything that Reason or Scripture forbids is sinful, and to refrain from doing it, if he refrain from doing it from reverence for the Eternal One, it is righteous. And to do things that are not prohibited in an even and proper way, is righteous.

Behold, then, all the actions of mankind are, without exception, either good or bad: and the intelligent man is he who weighs *all* his actions, before he does them, in this balance, and tests them with his best thought and the whole strength of his intellect, and chooses the best of them and forsakes all others. The sage (Ecclesiastes xii.) classifies all works as either good or bad. "For all works God will bring into judgment, over every hidden thing whether good or bad."

The Danger of Pride and Self-Righteousness

Many whose intention is to do right and serve God are not on their guard against things that destroy this service, and the cause of destruction enters, without their perceiving whence it comes. Thus, one of the Pious (Chassideem) said to his pupils: "If you had no iniquities, I should fear for you that which is greater than iniquities." They said to him: "What is greater than iniquities?" He replied: "Pride and haughtiness."

Man may strive to awaken his intelligence, so that it will make clear to him what the Creator has planted within his mind, by practising the praise of truth, contempt for falsehood, the choice of righteousness, and departure from iniquity.

(From The Gate of Humility.)

The Danger of Pride

The man who does good works is more likely to be overtaken by pride in them than by any other moral mischance; and its effect on conduct is injurious in the extreme. Therefore, among the most necessary of virtues is that one which banishes pride; and this is humility.

Humility, True and False

Humility is lowliness of the soul; and it is a quality of the soul that, when established there, allows its signs to be evident in the bodily members. The voice, for instance, is softened, and so is the language it utters; and one is subdued in times of anger, and vengeance is withheld when one has the power to avenge.

But there are three kinds of humility. One kind of humility is shared by man and by very many species of dumb animals; this is poverty of spirit and the sufferance of injuries that one has the power to avert. And this kind of humility is found in fools among the sons of men, and in low and ignorant people, on account of their want of knowledge and the weakness of their understanding. We are accustomed to call this humility, but it is, in truth, merely poverty of the soul and blind stupidity. But real humility is that which follows the exaltation of the soul after it has raised itself above sharing with the cattle their more shameful attributes. Then only, when humility and lowliness of soul are joined to such elevation, are they praiseworthy qualities.

The second variety of humility is humility towards men; either on account of their having dominion over us, or on account of our being in need of their services. This is submission in the right direction. But although it is proper, it is not a lasting quality; for it does not comprehend all reasonable beings, nor is such humility proper at all times and in all places.

But the third kind of humility is humility before the Creator, blessed be He, and its obligation embraces all reasonable beings, [8] and it is incumbent upon them at every time and in every place. This is the special kind of humility that I have in view. And all the Scriptural passages that speak of "the humble," "the meek," "the modest," "the brokenhearted," "the contrite," etc., etc., are written with reference to this third kind of humility — which is the most exalted degree of humility. Moreover, he that has acquired it is not far from the way that leads him near to God; and he will be favourably accepted by the Creator.

The Signs and Consequences of True Humility

Humility before the Creator obliges a man to behave meekly and unselfishly in all his transactions with his fellow-men, whether in matters of business or in any other relation of life.

The truly humble man will mourn for all the mistakes made by other men, and not triumph or rejoice over them.

Humility and Egotism

He who has true humility will be free from all pride, conceit, self-praise and self-glorification, even in his secret thoughts, when he is occupied in works of charity or other virtuous or righteous acts, whether commanded or not; and in his own soul he will account them as nothing in comparison to the greatness of his obligation to God.

Aids to the Cultivation of Humility

Among the aids to the cultivation of proper humility are the contemplation of the greatness of man's obligation to the Creator and the thought of how small is his fulfilment of his duties, whether those commanded by his own Reason or by Scripture. Another is contemplation of the wonders of the universe and on the insignificance of man in comparison with even this earth, while, in comparison with the greatness of the Creator, the whole universe, even the highest sphere, [9] is as nothing.

If a man fills his mind with these and similar thoughts, he will be continually humble, until humility has become a part of his very nature, and all pride and arrogance and haughtiness are removed from his heart, and this will deliver him from sin and error; as our sages, of blessed memory, say: "Think of three things and thou wilt never fall into sin; whence thou comest, whither thou goest, before whom thou hast to render an account."

The Charity of the Meek

He who is humble before God will not only do good to all men, but he will speak kindly to them and of them, and will never relate anything shameful about them, and will forgive them for any shameful things they may say about him, even if they are not worthy of such treatment. It is related of one of the *Chassideem,* that once when he was taking a walk with his disciples, they passed the carcass of a dog in an advanced stage of decomposition. His disciples exclaimed: "Oh, how this carcass stinks!" He replied: "Oh, how white its teeth are!" so as to counteract their remark.

If it be wrong to speak disparagingly of a dead dog, how much more so, of a living man; and if it be a merit to praise a dead dog for the whiteness of its teeth, how much more is it a duty to find out, and praise, the least merit in an intellectual human being? But it was also the intention of this pious man to teach his pupils to *habituate* themselves to speaking favourably, and to the avoidance of evil speaking. For that to which one accustoms the tongue becomes its natural speech.

Consistent Humility and Sincerity

He who is humble before God should be meek and modest in all the affairs of the world; both in what is seen and in what is secret; in his speech and in his actions; in his bodily activities, and when at rest; and what is in his heart and mind must not be the opposite to what is manifest about him; and all his actions must be well pondered and suitable, equal, equable, and constant, and must tend in the direction of humility and lowliness, both towards God and man...and our sages say, [10] "Be lowly of spirit in the presence of every man."

Where Humility is Sin

In matters of religion, justice, and of right and wrong, however, the meek will be high-spirited and fearless, punishing the wicked without fear or favour. He will never behave oppressively out of fear lest he might suffer oppression; but he will rescue the oppressed and help to bring him out of the power of the oppressor; and he will teach men to do right, and warn them against evil, to the utmost of his power.

The Hall-Marks of the Meek

First among the signs by which the meek are known is that they forgive all injuries and subdue their anger against those that treat them with contempt, even when they have the opportunity of avenging or resenting what has been done to them.

The second is, that when misfortunes come to them their endurance triumphs over their fear and grief, and they willingly submit to the decree of God, and own that His judgments are righteous.

The Pride Consistent with Humility

It may be asked: Can pride and humility dwell together in the heart? The answer requires a definition of pride.

There are two kinds of pride. Pride in the bodily powers and in corporeal and material things; and pride in spiritual and mental qualities, such as wisdom, and in good works. All pride of the former kind banishes humility. For all pride in the things of the world implies contempt for the Lord of all good, and ignorance of the instability of these things, and the rapidity with which they may depart, and shows that the proud man thinks he is, himself, his own benefactor, and that it is his own wisdom and his own power that has gained him the acquisitions of which he is proud.

Even pride in spiritual and mental qualities is of two kinds; one shameful, and the other admirable. The shameful kind is where a man prides himself on his wisdom and the righteousness of his conduct, and it leads to his being great in his own eyes and perfectly satisfied with himself, and to his thinking it enough if he gets a good name, and is praised among human beings; and it induces him to look with contempt on other men, and to despise them and talk against them; and to think little of the wise men of his day and of their greatness; and to glory in the failings of his fellows and in their folly. And this is what our sages mean by "glorifying one's self in the shame of one's neighbour."

The admirable kind of pride is that, when the wise man prides himself on his wisdom, and the just man on his works, he should acknowledge, in these things, the great beneficence of the Creator, and should rejoice on account of these gifts. Such pride in these gifts will then induce him to increase them and make good use of them, and to be meek with all around him; and to rejoice with his fellows, and be eager for their glory, and to cover over their folly, and to speak in praise of them, to love them, and to rejoice over them, and to be careful of their honour. Then, also, his own good deeds will appear so small in his eyes, that he will be continually striving to increase them. He will be humble because of his sense of inability to attain to the realisation of his ideal in respect to them, and he will be full of gratitude to God for giving him these precious qualities. Such pride is helpful, and not harmful, to humility.

Humility as a Worldly Advantage — Contentment

Humility is profitable to man in this world, because it makes him rejoice in his lot. For the whole world, and all it contains, is insufficient to satisfy the ambition of him into whom pride and a sense of greatness have entered, and he will look with contempt on whatever share of it falls to his lot; whereas, the humble man assigns no special rank to himself, but is content with whatever comes to him, and finds it sufficient. And this induces restfulness of soul, and minimises anxiety. He will eat what comes his way, and dress in the raiment that is readily found; and a small share of the world satisfies him.

The humble also bear troubles with greater fortitude than do the proud.

The Proper Study of Mankind is Man

Although it is incumbent upon us to investigate and study the whole universe, so as to understand the wisdom and goodness of the Creator, the subject most necessary to study, as well as the nearest and most obvious, is the evidence of divine wisdom shown in all that concerns the human species. For man is the universe in little (microcosm), and the proximate cause of the existence of the great world (macrocosm). And it is our duty to study the origin of man and his history; his birth, and the composition and structure of his component parts, and the members and organs of his body, their relations to each other, and the functions and purposes of every one of them; and the necessity of his being made as he is, in structure, form, and appearance. And then we must consider the objects of his being and all his mental qualities and characteristics, and the powers of his soul, and the light of his reason, and all the essentials and accidentals of his being, and his passions and desires, and his relation to the scheme of Creation.

From the standpoint of this study much of the mystery of the universe, and many of the secrets of this world, will become clear to us, because of the likeness of man to the world; and it has been said by some of the wise men that Philosophy is man's knowledge of himself: that is to say, such knowledge of man will enable us to recognise the Creator from the signs of His wisdom displayed in man. This is the meaning of what Job said: "And from my flesh I shall see God."

The tongue is the pen of the heart, and the messenger of the distant hidden soul.

• • • • • •

In speech one can see the superiority of man over the lower animals.

• • • • • •

It is the fools who think they know everything, and in their pride neglect that study of the world and man, which would compel gratitude to God, and life devoted to His service and the doing of good works.

When you have studied all that can be known of the universe, do not think that you know all about the wisdom and power of God. For in the world, we know, God has only manifested just so much of His wisdom and power as were necessary for the good of man. Not according to the reach of His wisdom and power is their manifestation in the phenomenal world (for they are infinite), but in accordance with the needs of His creation and of His creatures.

(From The Sixth Gate.)

Of Trust in God

Of all things the most necessary to him who would serve God, [11] is trust in God.

••••••

If one does not trust in God, one trusts in something, or in some one, else. And he who quits his trust otherwhere than in the One Eternal, removes God and His ruling providence from over him, and puts himself in the hands of that thing or person in whom he trusts.

••••••

He who trusts in his own wisdom or abilities, or in the strength of his body and in his own efforts, will labour in vain, weaken his powers, and find his skill inadequate to the attainment of his desires; ...and trust in wealth may be the destruction of the soul. He who trusts in God will be led to serve none other than Him, in that he will not build his hopes on a man, and will not wait, in anxious anticipation, for any human being; and he will not serve them, or try to curry favour with them; and he will not be hypocritical to please mankind, to the detriment of his service of God; and he will have no fear of man nor of human fault-finding. He will be independent, and strip off from himself the livery of human favours and benefactions.

••••••

He who trusts in God is able to turn his attention from worldly anxieties and devote it to doing what is right. For, in the restfulness of his soul and the liberty of his mind, and in the diminution of his anxieties in regard to worldly affairs, he may be compared to an alchemist who knows how to turn silver into gold and brass and tin to silver. Only that he is better off; for he needs neither implements nor materials in his alchemy, and he needs not store up his gold in fear of robbers, nor restrict his production to what is only enough for the day and be in fear for the morrow. For he has confidence that God will supply his wants when and where it may be requisite.

If he who trusts in God is wealthy, he will hasten cheerfully to fulfil all the religious and ethical obligations of wealth; and if he is without wealth, he will look upon its absence as a blessing from God, relieving him from the responsibilities its possession involves, and from the anxiety of guarding and administrating it.

The wealthy man who trusts in God will not find his wealth a hindrance to his faith; for he does not place his reliance upon his wealth, which is, in his eyes, trust money assigned to him for a limited period that he may apply it in various appointed

47

ways. He will not be proud, nor will he make any mention of his goodness to any one to whom he has been commanded to give some of this wealth, and he will not require any reward, or thanks, or praise; but he will render thanks to the Creator who has made him the agent of His beneficence. And if he loses his wealth he will not be anxious, or mourn its absence, but will be thankful to God at the taking away of what was only entrusted to him, just as he thanked God for the original gift; and he will rejoice in his portion, and not seek the injury of any one else, and not envy any other man his wealth.

The worldly advantages of trust in God include peace of mind from worldly anxieties, and rest for the soul from the disturbances of trouble caused by any want in the satisfaction of bodily appetites.

Keeping Account with the Soul

The keeping account with one's own soul is when a man busies himself in silent discussion between himself and his reason with the concerns of his religious and his worldly life, so that he may ascertain what are his spiritual and mental possessions, and what his obligations.

Every human being is bound, in proportion to his mental gifts, to keep account with his soul, and to calculate what service of heart and mind he owes the Creator. And more is required of those gifted with clearer perception, or who have been specially blessed, than from others; because both their debt of gratitude and their power of fulfilment are greater.

Among the many subjects of such contemplation, are the origin of one's own life, and the wonder of emergence from non-existence to existence, from nothingness to being, not on account of any superiority anticipated in man, but only by the kindness of God, and His goodness, and His free generosity. Thence it will be obvious to his reason that he has been considered more than all the animal and vegetable world, and raised in degree above all the rest of the material creation, and appointed to a more exalted destiny, and he will be conscious of his great obligation.

••••••

Such contemplation concerning the Deity and man's relation to the Creator, will show the duty of concentrating the heart on God's unity and spirituality, and on His service; so that there is no other thought or intention in all that one does, except to do it for the sake of God alone, with no thought of human praise or of the fear of man, or of advantages or of the removal of dangers, in this world or in a future state.

The service of God is of three kinds only:— Duties of the heart, such as are explained in this book; duties of the members and the heart together, such as prayer, the teaching of Scripture, and the teaching of Ethics [*lit.*, the teaching of wisdom, and commands of goodness, and prohibitions of evil]; and duties of the bodily members alone, such as the ceremonies of religion and the giving of charity. With these last the heart has nothing to do, except in so far as their intention and motive are concerned.

Contemplation Leading to Communion with God

If the believer will constantly meditate on the fact that the Creator sees all his thoughts and deeds, and will think it over with his own soul, the Creator will be constantly with him, and he will see Him with his mind's eye, and be in constant awe and reverence of Him; and he will examine all his conduct. And when this has become a constant habit of his mind, he will, helped by God, have reached the highest degree of the pious ones, and the most exalted rank of the righteous. He will not lack anything; nor will he choose anything more than the Creator has chosen for him. His will depends upon the will of the Creator, and his love on the love of the Creator; and that is loved by him which He loves, and that is contemned by him which is contemned by the Creator.

A man should commune with himself in reference to the desires of his heart and his worldly tastes; and a careful consideration of the ends they serve will lead him to look with contempt on ephemeral possessions; and his thoughts and desires will be fixed on the highest good, and on what is of eternal value to his mind and soul; and he will learn to strive only for what is barely necessary of the things of this world. He will desire to be kept from both poverty and riches, so that he may have enough for simple healthy life; and he will yearn after wisdom and spiritual possessions, of which no one can rob him.

Another subject for self-communing is the question as to whether we have made proper provision for the journey we must one day make, to another world, just as a traveller does not wait till he is on a journey before making provision for his necessities while travelling.

Another subject that should not be neglected, in the communing with one's own soul, is the inclination of the soul to seek the fellowship of the sons of men and the advantages of solitude and of separation from men, and the evil of associating ourselves with their follies when we are not forced to do so. Too much talking is calculated to lead to the talking of slander and the telling of lies, and even to the taking of false oaths. One of the *Chassideem* said to his disciples: "The *Torah* permits our swearing by the name of the Creator to what is true, but I counsel you not to take an oath by the holy name of God, whether to the truth or to a lie. Say simply 'Yes,' or 'No.' Too much social intercourse also leads to boasting and displaying one's knowledge.

The pure of heart will always love solitude. But here again the temptation to complete solitude must also be guarded against. For the society of philosophers, the pious, and of great men, is of great advantage.

One should also consider well, in communing with his soul, whether he has made the best use of any wealth that he may possess, doing good with it. And he should meditate also on the many ways in which one man can help another; and consider that he should love for others what he loves for himself, and hate for others what he hates for himself, rejoicing in their joy and grieving at their sorrow. And he should be full of compassion for them, and ward off from them, to the utmost of his power, anything that may injure them; as it is said (Levit. xix.), "And thou shalt love thy neighbour as thyself."

The Gate of Love

The intention of all separation from the world is only so that one may concentrate the whole heart upon the one object of love for the Creator, and that one may be filled with longing to fulfil His will. This perfect love of God is the primary aim and intention, as well as the end and fulfilment, of all obligations taught by Reason, by Scripture, or by Tradition.

••••••

This love of God is the yearning of the soul for the Creator, and her turning, of her own accord, towards Him, so that she may be united with His light, which is the highest. That is, that the soul, which is herself pure spirit, inclines, more than any other spiritual being, to her like, and in her very nature recedes from that which is her opposite:—from gross matter.

They who love God will do all that is right, without the hope of reward, and will forsake all that is evil, without the fear of punishment. They will also have no fear of anything, or of any person, in this or any other world, except of the Creator alone. And they will be indifferent to the praise and blame of men in doing the will of God. They will be pure in body as well as in mind, and fly from evil deeds of all kinds. They will serve the Creator not only in obedience to the laws of revelation, some of which are only binding in given circumstances, but also in the duties that are commanded by Reason and Conscience, and with every good spiritual quality.

Notes

[1] The word here used is *Torah* (see next note).

[2] *Torah,* literally guide, instruction, but generally translated "Law," is a word used in Hebrew literature with several distinct meanings:— (1) The Pentateuch, as distinguished from the rest of the Bible; (2) Scripture, any part of the O.T., as distinguished from The Talmud Rabbinic opinions and traditions; (3) The *Contents* of the Bible and Talmud, together with scientific, medical, ethical, or other facts or theories, studied for the purpose of elucidating the spiritual meaning, or practical application, of the Mosaic Law; (3a)

the habit of studying *Torah* in the sense (3), *i.e.*, Religion, hygiene and ethics, etc., based upon principles traceable to the Pentateuch.

[3] This is the literal translation of *nichsof;* comp, *kestph,* silver.

[4] The Rabbis frequently used this term for God. Hashem = THE name, *i.e.*, the Divine name of four letters, derived from *hajah,* to exist, which was thought too sacred to pronounce in common speech, and the meaning of which connotes absolute, infinite existence.

[5] Bachye is only following many Hebraists, and not at all straining the sense, when he renders "Shemang," in this verse, "Understand," or hearken, instead of "hear."

[6] See note 2.

[7] Note that not the act but its motive determines its ethical significance.

[8] *Kol hammedaberim*, a phrase often used by our author, means, literally, all who speak or arrange words in order, or are capable of logic.

[9] In summarising, I have, here, been careful not to modernise the *form* of B's thought too much. Of course, its substance is as valid now as in the days of the Copernican astronomy.

[10] Wherever this phrase occurs it refers to the Rabbis whose sayings are preserved in the Talmud.

[11] It must be remembered that Bachye regards moral virtues, and all righteous conduct, as part of the service of God.